MW00423048

WOMAN
IN THE MIRROR

Ungodly Soul Ties:
Break Free to Break Through

TARSHA L. CAMPBELL

Cover & Interior Design: Tarsha L. Campbell

Edited by: Donna L. Ferrier

Proofread by: Mellissa Thomas

Cover stock photos: Photodune

Author's Photo: Michael Cairns

Published by:
DOMINIONHOUSE Publishing & Design, LLC
P.O. Box 681938 | Orlando, Florida 32868
407.703.4800 phone/fax | www.mydominionhouse.com

****

The Lord gave the word: great was the company of those
that published it. (Psalms 68:11)

Acknowledgments

Special thanks to:
My wonderful husband, Dwayne Campbell,
my awesome mom, Pastor Betty Jamison,
my dear brother, Canice Okoro,
my amazing sisters, Anita Neal-Okoro and
Christine Lombard. Thank you for your positive
feedback and taking time to make sure
the message in this book was
clear and on point.

Much thanks to my pastors,
Bishop Mark & Pastor Ruth Chironna.
Your dedication and commitment to the family of
Church on the Living Edge and the Body of Christ
at large, inspires me to empower others with
love, integrity, and compassion,
in order to bring them hope.

Last, but certainly not least,
to Tanya Marie Lewis, my brilliant sister
and business twin. Thank you for being my
accountability partner for this project.
We reached our goals! Yay!!

DEDICATION

This book is dedicated to every person
who desires to break free from
ungodly soul ties, draw closer to God,
realize their full potential,
and fulfill their purpose and destiny.
May you find your true identity in the
Father and be empowered
with His greatness.

Your time for a breakthrough is here!

-T.L. Campbell

TABLE OF CONTENTS

TABLE OF CONTENTS

"When you know your

true identity in God,

you can overcome any

obstacle and experience

divine breakthrough in

any area of your life."

-T.L. Campbell

"The mirror of life

doesn't always reveal

what you want to see.

Sometimes it

reveals death cycles

that sabotage

your ultimate success

and happiness."

-T.L. Campbell

CHAPTER 1

INTRODUCTION: WHO IS THE WOMAN IN THE MIRROR?

As we embark upon this journey to liberation and healing, I'm so excited about the entire *Woman in the Mirror Empowerment Series*™. The books in this series are all about helping you experience a divine breakthrough in your life so you can walk in your God-given identity, achieve your full potential, and live a fulfilled life. If you haven't read the first book in the series,

Woman in the Mirror: A Case of Mistaken Identity, I encourage you to do so. In that book I share:

1. The importance of reacquainting yourself with your originator, Father God, on a more intimate level and the benefits of doing so.

2. What self-image, self-worth, and self-esteem are.

3. How the enemy (Satan) distorts your God-given identity to keep you from your divine identity, potential, purpose, and destiny.

I also help you, as the woman in the mirror, identify ways you can become a victim of a case of mistaken identity.

In total, there are ten life-altering teachings in *The Woman in the Mirror Empowerment Series*™. Each teaching presents a different God-given prophetic vision of a woman engaged in some type of activity as she's standing in front of a mirror. Her actions, as reflected in the mirror, represent her disposition or state of mind either physically, emotionally, spiritually, or a combination of all three. The woman in the mirror represents a state you and I may find ourselves in during various seasons of our lives.

Not only can the woman in the mirror represent you and me as individuals, she can also represent a body of people, such as "the church" or a country like the United States, which are frequently described as women. That being said, the revelatory teachings in

The Woman in the Mirror Empowerment Series™ can bring transformation into the lives of both women and men and make a tremendous impact in all segments of society.

Although I designed each book in the series as a stand-alone publication so you can reap the benefits of each one independently, I encourage you to read all of them to experience ultimate freedom and emancipation from the strategies of the enemy that impede your growth in God, set limitations in your life, and keep you in bondage to consistent death cycles.

So let's move forward now and explore what the Holy Spirit wants to share in this powerful teaching about ungodly soul ties and achieving divine breakthrough! Are you ready?

Mirror, Mirror on the Wall

A Moment to Reflect

What do you see when you look in the mirror?

How do you see yourself?

What are some of the negative thought patterns in your life that sabotage your progress?

"When you are ready

to acknowledge the

strongholds in your life,

you are ready to find

true freedom."

-T.L. Campbell

CHAPTER 2

GET READY FOR
YOUR BREAKTHROUGH

I don't know if you have sensed a shift in the Spirit over recent years, but God is getting ready to release His people into a greater level of anointing, power, and authority. For some time now, I have been hearing the word *acceleration*. That's right, *acceleration*. God is speeding some things up for those in the Spirit who have both positioned and opened themselves to receive from Him in this hour.

I don't know about you, but I want every good and perfect gift God has for me. This is why I am positioning not only my physical body, but I am also aligning my mind with the will and purpose of God for my life. This means I am getting rid of negative dispositions, mindsets, and attitudes that will hinder me from reaching my God-given destiny. I want to encourage you to do the same.

Destiny is calling you. You do know you have a destiny, don't you? We all have a destiny. Webster's Dictionary defines destiny as "a predetermined course." We all have a place we must reach, a destiny, a predetermined course.

By His Spirit, God began revealing to me what destiny was when I wrote my book, *Five Qualities of a Woman of Destiny*. Here's how

He defined destiny to me. Are you ready for this? *"Destiny is a God-appointed person, going to a God-appointed place, at a God-appointed time, for a God-appointed purpose."* Isn't that a great definition?

I have an appointment with destiny. You have an appointment with destiny. God also revealed, however, that a lot of people are going to miss their appointment with destiny, because they have not spiritually positioned themselves in the right place. In order for you and me to reach our appointed place of destiny, we must experience a breakthrough.

Breakthrough is another interesting word. It means "a significant dramatic overcoming of a perceived obstacle," which means you can see and feel the obstacle. It's all around you. It's in front of you. It's presenting itself as an insurmountable object designed to keep you from your destiny.

When God revealed to me that I needed my own personal breakthrough, He first showed me I needed to break loose from some things. This may be true for you, too. You've got to break loose from those things that have held you back and continue to hold you back from your destiny, and from living the life God has for you. If you can, say this out loud: "Break free to break through." Say it one more time: "Break free to break through!"

Paul says it like this in Romans 7:24 (KJV): "Oh wretched man that I am! Who shall deliver me from the body of this death?" The Amplified Bible records Paul as saying it like this: "O unhappy [and] pitiable [and] wretched man that I am! Who will release [and] deliver me from [the shackles of] this body of death?"

I like the way the verse reads in the Amplified Bible, especially the part that says, "this body of death." When I began to study this particular phrase, I discovered it referred to a horrible practice of the ancient Romans. When they tortured someone, they tied a dead body around a living man's neck and forced the live person to drag the dead body around everywhere he went.

Can you imagine the torment of carrying a dead, rotting corpse tied around your neck? Not only would you see the rotting flesh and smell the stench everywhere you went, but also the longer you carried this dead weight, the more the rotting flesh would contaminate you until death came upon you, too. Can you say, "Break free to break through"?

By now you may be seeing a picture as it relates to the subject of ungodly soul ties. Can you see this dead weight in your mind? Can you see yourself carrying it around everywhere you go? God is going to speak to you about this rotting flesh you're carrying around as we continue to unfold the liberating truth contained within this installment of the *Woman in the Mirror Empowerment Series*™.

When I began writing *Woman in the Mirror: Ungodly Soul Ties – Break Free to Break Through*, God revealed a powerful word of prophecy:

My people are tied to things that keep them from experiencing true intimacy with Me and fullness of life. Many have tied themselves to a person, a group, an event, a thing, an institution, and even belief systems, which have become bodies of death in their lives. These "bodies of death" are ungodly soul ties that have incapacitated my people; held them in bondage; and kept them from reaching their destiny, their purpose. They can't flow; they can't grow; they can't move; and they can't go.

Many hear My voice. They have dreams and even see visions. They have received words of prophecy and I have declared My promises over their lives. Some are even faithful to read My Word, the Bible.

Some even pay their tithes and give their offerings. But many are unknowingly being held back by ungodly soul ties that only serve as dead weights to keep them from rising to true intimacy with Me. Without deliverance from these ungodly soul ties, they will never lead abundant lives.

It's unattainable. They can see it. They see other people living it, but they won't be able to reach it, grasp it, and become all I envision for their lives because these dead weights, these bodies of death tied around their necks, are causing them to experience death cycles themselves. Their minds, their wills, and their emotions are tied to that which is corrupt and perverted and form strongholds that imprison them. But I, the Lord, say to you today, there must be a release in order for My purpose in your life to be fulfilled. I'm declaring a day of independence this day for you. Breakthrough is at hand. It's within your grasp. Receive your breakthrough through the word today.

Wow! What a word from the Lord. This word of prophecy speaks volumes. It's a resounding promise of freedom. When I first heard this word from the Lord, it stirred in my heart and I wanted to hear more about these ungodly soul ties that were keeping me from being all God purposed me to be. Does this word have the same effect on you? If so, keep reading. What the Lord revealed about this subject will fundamentally shift your life as it has shifted my life and many others. Let's delve into the meat of this revolutionizing truth.

Mirror, Mirror on the Wall
A Moment to Reflect

List three areas in your life where you need a serious breakthrough.

What will your breakthroughs look like when they happen in your life?

"The mirror represents

a place where you

experience true intimacy

with God. The more you

enter into true intimacy

with God, the more

He begins to reveal the

destiny He has for you."

-T.L. Campbell

Chapter 3

The Woman In The Mirror Revealed

The woman, as prophetically revealed in this book, *Ungodly Soul Ties – Break Free to Break Through*, is standing in front of a mirror and she has a belt tied around her waist. Attached to the belt are ropes of various lengths. The mirror represents a place where she experiences true intimacy with God. The apparent goal of the woman, as the vision unfolds, is to draw closer to the mirror in an effort to draw closer to God in greater intimacy. The more she becomes truly intimate with God, the more the Father (her originator) reveals who she really is in Him, and all He has purposed, planned, and predestined for her life.

Intimacy can be conveyed in this simple way: in-to-me-you-see. The more you enter into true intimacy with God, the more He begins to reveal the destiny He has for you. And because the "I AM" God made you in His likeness, He reveals the real you as you continue to see yourself in His mirror. For more about this subject, read volume one in the series: *Woman in the Mirror: A Case of Mistaken Identity*.

So we see that the woman facing the mirror is trying to draw closer to Father God in greater intimacy. For she knows if she continues to do so she will grow and progress in Him. She has a problem, however. While she can see the reflection of the destiny God has for her in the mirror, and all He desires her to be, she has some ropes of various lengths tied to the belt around her waist that keep pulling her in every direction as she tries to draw closer to God, to her purpose, and to her destiny. They are pulling her here, pulling her there, and pulling her out of the will of God. The Spirit revealed to me that the various lengths of each rope represent past and present ungodly soul ties the woman remains connected to.

Every time this woman in the mirror tries to take three steps toward divine fulfillment, disappointment and disillusionment pull her four steps back. Every time she makes a move to embark upon a new business venture, she is pulled back to square one where she feels the agony of defeat and extreme failure. Every time she feels her new relationship might just work out this time, she is blindsided by betrayal and unfaithfulness. Every time she makes up her mind to step out in obedience to God's voice to launch her ministry, relentless fear grips her heart, and she remains paralyzed year in and year out.

Does any of this sound familiar? Are you this woman in the mirror?

This woman in the mirror so vividly describes the vicious cycle many people face today. This was the cycle I was in. This is why I understand it all too well. Year in and year out, every time I thought I was growing, flowing, and going, I eventually found myself snatched back out of the presence, purpose, and will of God. Divine success and fulfillment were constantly eluding me, and I couldn't understand why. I was doing all the right things: reading my Bible, paying my tithes, and giving my offerings, all in an effort to draw closer to God in greater intimacy, but certain aspects of my life were still barren and desolate.

When God revealed to me the vision of the woman in the mirror I just described, along with the devastating effects of ungodly soul ties, my whole life turned around. More importantly, death cycles and generational curses in my family tree were broken off my life. Do you need death cycles broken off your life? Do you need a breakthrough? Well, today is your day and the first key is identifying the ungodly soul ties that are hindering your growth and progress.

A KEY THING TO KNOW IN THIS STUDY:
God created man as a three part being. Man is a spirit, he has a soul, and these two parts are housed in his physical body. I Thess. 5:23

"It's very important to

be connected to the right

people, things, and mindset

to get to your next level.

That's why it's so crucial that

you allow the LORD to show

you who to connect with in

certain seasons of

your life."

-T.L. Campbell

CHAPTER 4

WHAT ARE SOUL TIES? THE GOOD, THE BAD, THE UGLY

At this point, you might be asking, "What's a soul tie, Tarsha?" The following definition I didn't read in a dictionary or book. Most of the time, I try not to read books first when I feel God wants to speak to me, because I want to hear directly what the Spirit of God wants to say to me about a given subject. Once He speaks, I then compare notes with other reputable sources to see if what I heard is on target. So this is how the Spirit defined a soul tie to me: "a soulish connection in which you engage your mind, your will, and your emotions with a person, a group, an event, an ideology, or a belief system." Soul ties involve completely engaging your entire soul with another person or a group of people, such as your church, family, coworkers, sorority, etc.; an event, such as a marriage, divorce, or a memory; or an ideology, such as a paradigm, perception, or a belief system. You can tie yourself to negative thought patterns, such as, "I can only get this far"; "I'm too fat, so I can only obtain so much in life"; or "I only have this level of education." In other words, soul ties can be formed with anyone or anything you've given your mind, your will, and your emotions to. A simpler definition for what your soul is – it's your mind, will, and emotions.

Not all soul ties are bad, however. As the Holy Spirit revealed to me, "A good soul tie is a mutually beneficial connection that serves to uplift, encourage, and advance the will and purpose of God in your life." So good soul ties are helpful connections that lead to positive progression in your life, especially regarding God's will and purpose for you.

Good connections and relationships are necessary to help advance the fulfillment of God's purpose in your life. It's crazy to think you can advance in life all by yourself. Even Jesus connected Himself with twelve men to help advance the will and purpose of God in His life, and He was God manifested in the flesh.

What can really trip us up is thinking we don't need one another. Satan would love for me say, "I don't need my sister. I have just as much as she has. I've been to college; I have a degree. I don't need my family anymore. I don't need my church," and these lies of Satan go on and on. But because we let pride take residence in our hearts, we tell ourselves, "I'll do fine on my own. I don't need her; I don't need him; and I *certainly* don't need them." At that point, we unknowingly respond to Satan's strategies, lies, and schemes, by breaking our good connections, our good soul ties. But we need good soul ties to grow and progress in God.

David and Jonathan's relationship is a biblical example of a good soul tie. I Samuel 18:1 (KJV) states that David's heart was knitted to the heart of Jonathan: "And it came to pass, when he had made an end of speaking unto Saul, that the soul of Jonathan was knit with the soul of David, and Jonathan loved him as his own soul."

God had anointed David to be king; He had a divine purpose and will for his life, but David needed Jonathan to help him advance the will and purpose God had placed in him. Jonathan was a king's kid, raised in the king's palace, so he had spent time in the kingdom and understood kingdom protocol. In other words, Jonathan knew how to operate in the kingdom.

David wasn't raised in a palace. David was in the backfields with the lions, the sheep, and the bears. So he needed Jonathan to show him how to flow in the kingdom because God wanted to position David to be Israel's king. Therefore, God strategically placed Jonathan in David's life to help advance His will and purpose. I'm sure David added to Jonathan's life, too. David, being a worshipper, most likely taught Jonathan how to draw closer to the Heavenly Father in greater intimacy. This was truly a mutually beneficial connection! Both parties involved had something to bring to the table. The relationship wasn't a one way street. A telltale sign of a good soul tie is everyone involved in the relationship grows and progress in some way.

Before moving on to another example of a good biblical soul tie, I want to ask you a question. Who has God placed in your life during this season that will help you prepare for your royal assignment? And since we are talking about mutually beneficial relationships, who has the Father allowed you to connect with to help that other person prepare or complete his or her God-given assignment?

As a life, destiny, and empowerment coach, I am consistently encouraging my clients to be conscious of what's going on around them and who's playing a specific role in their lives at specific times. God might have given you the connection you need to prepare and escort you into your next God-given assignment and purpose, just like He did for David. Who has God placed in your life to help you start or operate your own business? Or, has He placed you in someone else's life to help him or her in that way? Who has God placed in your life to help you launch your ministry or community organization? Or, has He placed you in someone else's life to help him or her reach that goal? Who has God placed in your life to help you be a better parent, spouse, or friend? Or, has He placed you in someone else's life to help him or her reach a similar goal? Who has God placed in your life to help you become a better boss, employee or team player? Or, has He placed you in someone else's life to help him or her do the same? These are only a handful of reasons we need good soul ties in our lives, and I personally thank God for the good soul ties in my life!

Ruth's relationship with Naomi is another example of a good biblical soul tie. Let's get a little glimpse into how God connected these two women, beginning with Ruth 1:5-8 and 14-19 (NLT):

> 5 Both Mahlon and Kilion died. This left Naomi alone, without her two sons or her husband.
>
> 6 Then Naomi heard in Moab that the Lord had blessed his people in Judah by

giving them good crops again. So Naomi and her daughters-in-law got ready to leave Moab to return to her homeland.

7 With her two daughters-in-law she set out from the place where she had been living, and they took the road that would lead them back to Judah.

8 But on the way, Naomi said to her two daughters-in-law, "Go back to your mothers' homes. And may the Lord reward you for your kindness to your husbands and to me.

Jumping down to verse 14…

14 And again they wept together, and Orpah kissed her mother-in-law goodbye. But Ruth clung tightly to Naomi.

15 "Look," Naomi said to her, "your sister-in-law has gone back to her people and to her gods. You should do the same."

16 But Ruth replied, "Don't ask me to leave you and turn back. Wherever you go, I will go; wherever you live, I will live. Your people will be my people, and your God will be my God.

17 Wherever you die, I will die, and there I will be buried. May the Lord punish me severely if I allow anything but death to separate us!"

18 When Naomi saw that Ruth was determined to go with her, she said nothing more.

19 So the two of them continued on their journey. When they came to Bethlehem, the entire town was excited by their arrival. "Is it really Naomi?" the women asked.

This Bible passage opens by painting a grim picture of the extreme devastation that had come into the lives of Naomi and her two daughters-in-law, Ruth and Orpah. All three women had lost their beloved husbands, and they were dwelling in a land plagued by extreme famine. So Naomi said to her grieving daughters-in-law, "Why don't you just go back to your people?" The Bible stated while Orpah decided to leave her mother-in-law, Ruth clung to her.

By the Spirit, Ruth knew there was a purpose for her life that couldn't be achieved among her own people, the Moabites. Somehow Ruth knew Naomi was tied to her destiny. In order for her to reach it, however, she had to make a conscious decision to make a new connection. So Ruth had to leave her former connections and join with a woman who was going to take her to her destiny and open the door to her purpose.

As a result of this divine connection, God dramatically changed the lives of both these women for the better. According to Matthew 1:5-16, Ruth and Naomi's connection with the Kinsman Redeemer, Boaz, tied them to the lineage of Jesus Christ, the Savior of the world. Their relationship, therefore, was a good soul tie and a Godly soul tie, used to advance the will and purpose of God in the lives of all parties involved.

Now I want us to focus on the flip side of Godly soul ties – ungodly soul ties – because my goal is to see you break free to break through. The Spirit expressed to me that an ungodly soul tie is "an unbalanced, twisted, perverted soulish connection." To say it is unbalanced means one side is tipping more than the other. One person is giving more than the other. One is taking more and leaving the other person depleted. Someone is draining you of your anointing, your time, your knowledge, your resources, and your emotional strength, just like a spiritual leech. You know what a leech is, don't you? It's a parasitic organism that sucks the blood/ life out of its host organism without giving anything in return.

You and I can encounter people and situations that literally suck the life out of us spiritually, emotionally, physically, financially, etc. My friend, that's what an ungodly soul tie will do to you! It's MO is to restrain, drain, and control some or all of the parties involved. Depending on who or what you're tied to, an ungodly soul tie can manifest itself as nothing more than a big game of control and manipulation, much like a puppet master pulling the strings on a puppet.

As you are hearing this definition of an ungodly soul tie, does it ring a bell in your spirit and send an alert message to your soul? When the

Holy Spirit first revealed the definition of an ungodly soul tie to me, I started thinking of all the different people and situations in my life that fit this definition like a finely tailored suit. I said to myself, "Oh my God, this is the problem! This is an ungodly soul tie."

The big problem with ungodly soul ties is that they hinder the growth, the advancement, and the will of God in the lives of those connected. You can be connected with certain people, groups of people, events, ideologies, concepts, and belief systems that can drain the life out of you and keep you from growing and advancing in God's will for your life. You can be doing all the right things – paying your tithes, giving your offerings, reading your Bible, and serving God the best you know how – but if you are connected to the wrong thing, you may still find yourself in a state of utter barrenness, unable to produce to the capacity you know you can, and the way God has predestined you to.

In your dreams you can see yourself doing great things and having God's highest and best. You might have even received special prophetic words about all the wonderful things God desires to give you. At this point, you're up to your neck in promises from God, but something keeps pulling you away time and time again, impeding your growth and hindering your progress. *Does this sound familiar?*

I hope you can hear what the Spirit is saying today. You're that woman trying to behold all she sees in God's mirror of purpose and destiny.

It's you! You're reaching and grasping, trying to obtain what the Father said is rightfully yours, but these twisted and perverted ungodly soul ties are pulling you in every direction and hindering you from reaching the new dimensions and realms that God has prepared for you. They are keeping you from advancing in God's will and purpose for your life.

It's very important to be connected to the right people, things, and mindset to get to your next dimension. That's why it's so crucial that you allow the LORD to show you who to connect with in certain seasons of your life. Many times we try to hang on to people, to a group, or to an event past the season we're supposed to be connected with him, her, them, or it.

When that happens, at some point the relationship gets twisted, even to the point of crossing the line into perversion, and it stunts your growth. And because the season of being with that particular person or that particular group has passed, the relationship or the connection gets out of balance, out of order, and out of God's will. So instead of going straight on, you're leaning and completely off course. In many instances, you cease to experience any type of growth at all. Then you end up spiritually regressing, because you are out of balance. Out of balance leads to out of order. Out of order leads to misalignment with God's will. Being out of alignment with God's will leads to complete frustration and stagnation.

Because God is a God of order, a God of purpose, a God of times, and a God of seasons, He will cause a break in the relationship, and you and the other party will go your separate ways. God, as a loving and gracious Father, will cause some kind of event to happen where you're not with that person anymore just so both of you can grow. Can you say, "Break free to break through?"

Now You Know
Below are more biblical examples of Godly and ungodly soul ties:

Godly Soul Ties:
Mary and Elisabeth - Luke 1
Paul and Silas - Acts 16:19-34
Paul and Timothy - I Timothy 1

Ungodly Soul Ties:
Ahab and Jezebel - I Kings 16:29-33
Samson and Delilah - Judges 16:4-31

"Being entangled in an ungodly soul tie can be a two-way street...you have to acknowledge which role you have played in order to sever the ungodly tie and break free to break through."

-T.L. Campbell

CHAPTER 5

HOW ARE
UNGODLY SOUL TIES FORMED?

Now that you know what ungodly soul ties are and what they look like, your next question will probably be, "How are all these ungodly soul ties developed?" Let's go to II Samuel 13. This is where God began speaking to me about the ungodly soul ties in my life. He used the main character of this scripture passage, Tamar, to reveal to me some powerful and enlightening things about ungodly soul ties and the devastating grip they can have on a person's life.

In this particular passage, the Spirit revealed to me three strands that make up the ungodly soul tie. The number three is significant because Ecclesiastes 4:12 says, "a threefold cord is not quickly broken." God works in threes: Father, Son, Holy Spirit; birth, death, resurrection. But for every divine kingdom model there's also a satanic system that models itself in the same way, for the kingdom of darkness has it's ungodly trinity: the dragon, the beast, and the false prophet. So Satan works in threes, too. This is why breaking an ungodly soul tie isn't always easy because it's also comprised of three strands.

In II Samuel 13:1-20, we read about the tragic story of Tamar and her family – how things became twisted – leaving her desolate and unfulfilled all the days of her life and in need of a divine breakthrough. Let's read this story together. The passage is a little lengthy, but it's worth reading to get a clear picture of the negative dynamics in Tamar's life.

1 And it came to pass that after this, that Absalom the son of David had a fair sister, whose name was Tamar; and Amnon the son of David loved her.

2 And Amnon was so vexed, that he fell sick for his sister Tamar; for she [was] a virgin; and Amnon thought it hard for him to do anything to her.

3 But Amnon had a friend, whose name [was] Jonadab, the son of Shimeah David's brother: and Jonadab [was] a very subtle man.

4 And he said unto him, Why [art] thou, [being] the king's son, lean from day to day? Wilt thou not tell me? And Amnon said unto him, I love Tamar, my brother Absalom's sister.

5 And Jonadab said unto him, Lay thee down on thy bed, and make thyself sick: and when thy father cometh to see thee, say unto him, I pray thee, let my sister Tamar come, and give me meat, and dress the meat in my sight, that I may see [it], and eat [it] at her hand.

6 So Amnon lay down, and made himself sick: and when the king was come to see him, Amnon said unto the king, I pray thee, let Tamar my sister come, and make me a couple of cakes in my sight, that I may eat at her hand.

7 Then David sent home to Tamar, saying, Go now to thy brother Amnon's house, and dress him meat.

8 So Tamar went to her brother Amnon's house; and he was laid down. And she took flour, and kneaded [it], and made cakes in his sight, and did bake the cakes.

9 And she took a pan, and poured [them] out before him; but he refused to eat. And Amnon said, Have out all men from me. And they went out every man from him.

10 And Amnon said unto Tamar, Bring the meat into the chamber, that I may eat of thine hand. And Tamar took the cakes which she had made, and brought [them] into the chamber to Amnon her brother.

11 And when she had brought [them] unto him to eat, he took hold of her, and said unto her, Come lie with me, my sister.

12 And she answered him, Nay, my brother, do not force me; for no such thing ought to be done in Israel: do not thou this folly.

13 And I, whither shall I cause my shame to go? And as for thee, thou shalt be as one of the fools in Israel. Now therefore, I pray thee, speak unto the king; for he will not withhold me from thee.

14 Howbeit he would not hearken unto her voice: but, being stronger than she, forced her, and lay with her.

15 Then Amnon hated her exceedingly; so that the hatred wherewith he hated her

[was] greater than the love wherewith he had loved her. And Amnon said unto her, Arise, be gone.

16 And she said unto him, [There] is no cause: this evil in sending me away [is] greater than the other that thou didst unto me. But he would not hearken unto her.

17 Then he called his servant that ministered unto him, and said, Put now this [woman] out from me, and bolt the door after her.

18 And [she had] a garment of divers colours upon her: for with such robes were the king's daughters that were virgins appareled. Then his servant brought her out, and bolted the door after her.

19 And Tamar put ashes on her head, and rent her garment of divers colours that [was] on her, and laid her hand on her head, and went on crying.

20 And Absalom her brother said unto her, Hath Amnon thy brother been with thee? But hold now thy peace, my sister: he [is] thy brother; regard not this thing. So Tamar remained desolate in her brother Absalom's house.

In this story we have Tamar, King David's daughter. Tamar had so much to look forward to. She was royalty and a princess in her father's kingdom. Tamar was very special and she was a virgin. Unbeknownst to her, Tamar had an admirer, but this was a problem because the admirer was her half or stepbrother, Amnon.

Both Tamar and Amnon shared the same father, King David, but they had different mothers.

Amnon had a strong desire for his sister, Tamar. He really wanted her and was driven by his passions so deeply that he began to call his feelings for his sister "love." As you will see later, though, his alleged love was actually lust. He had her so much in his spirit that it began to show on his outward appearance. Even those around him began to say, "Man, what's wrong with you? You're the king's son; why are you so down? Why have you stopped eating?" Amnon was convinced that he loved Tamar.

So one of his friends, Jonadab (who was actually his cousin) said, "Hey, man, you don't have to go through all that. You're a king's kid. I've got a plan for you." You see, his friend was a deceitful man; he was accustomed to using trickery to get what he desired. Jonadab convinced Amnon if he really wanted Tamar, all he had to do was go after her by any means necessary. Jonadab said to Amnon, "Why don't you just lay down in your chamber and tell your dad that you need Tamar to come see about your needs?"

So Amnon laid himself down, acting as if he was sick, and his father, David, came in and asked him, "What do you want? What do you need? Cough medicine? Do you need to go to the doctor? Did you take your flu shot this year?"

Amnon responded, "No, Dad; all I need is Tamar."

I don't know why David couldn't see what was going on, (maybe he wasn't tuned in to the Spirit at that time), but he sent his daughter into the lion's den. Tamar was probably around fifteen years of age and very naïve, so when she arrived at Amnon's house, she didn't know what was going on. All she knew was her father, the king, sent her to Amnon's house to do a job. So she went inside and began to make the bread in the presence of Amnon and all the servants who were there. Tamar didn't see any harm, because Amnon's servants were there; what did she have to worry about? Besides, Amnon wasn't a stranger; he wasn't some pervert that we'd hear about on the six o'clock news today. He wasn't one of those dirty old men in the corner, saying, "Come here; let me see what you've got." Amnon was her brother. *She was in safe hands, right?*

63

When Tamar was getting ready to give Amnon the bread, he said, "No, I want it a certain way." So he sent all his servants out of the room and asked Tamar to come into his private chamber and serve what she had prepared. Only when poor Tamar went to go feed the bread to Amnon did he reveal his true identity and motives. I can just hear Amnon now as he said to Tamar, "I'm not sick...I'm not hungry...I just want you."

The First Strand of an Ungodly Soul Tie

As Amnon's plan against his sister unfolds, the first strand of an ungodly soul tie is revealed, and it is *lust*. Lust can be defined as an intense desire or longing. When most of us hear the word "lust" we only think in terms of sexual lust, like an intense longing for a person you're attracted to, such as a boyfriend or a first love.

When dealing with an ungodly soul tie, however, sexual lust isn't the only kind of lust, although you or someone you're connected to may be dealing with this type of lust within the relationship. The Holy Spirit showed me, even in my own life, that a person can have an intense desire and longing for all sorts of things that are not necessarily good for them.

We can have an intense desire or longing for acceptance, for example. We can have an intense desire or longing for approval, always needing to be validated by someone else. We can be so driven by such desires that we always need everyone's "thumbs up" before we even make a move. You or the person(s) you're in a relationship with can even have an intense desire or longing for control.

We're talking about breaking free to break through. As we move deeper into this powerful and liberating teaching, I want to ask you to allow the Holy Spirit to shine His light in the areas of your life where you have been entangled with ungodly soul ties. Also be mindful that as more light is shed, the LORD may reveal to you that you're either a perpetrator or a victim of an ungodly soul tie (or both).

Being entangled in an ungodly soul tie can be a two-way street. Like Tamar, you can easily find yourself caught up in another person's madness. In any instance, you have to acknowledge which role you have played in order to sever the ungodly tie and break free to break through. We'll talk more about that later. For now let's focus on getting a clear picture of the three strands of an ungodly soul tie.

The Second Strand of an Ungodly Soul Tie

The second strand of an ungodly soul tie is *perversion*. Because Amnon was driven by his unwarranted and unbridled passion for his sister, he perverted his relationship with her. When Amnon raped Tamar, he sinned against God by breaking the written law in Leviticus 18:11 (NTL): "Do not have sexual relations with your stepsister, the daughter of any of your father's wives, for she is your sister."

In II Samuel 13:11-12 it says that Amnon took hold of Tamar. The phrase "took hold of" has two meanings in Hebrew (the original language it was written in). One carries a positive connotation, the other a negative. The positive connotation means "to aid, to mend, to encourage, to fortify"; the negative means "to hold fast upon, to seize, to hold, to bind."

As a brother, Amnon should have been treating Tamar like a sister: fortifying her, building her up, mending her, encouraging her, and strengthening her as a good soul tie. Instead he seized her, bound her, and wrapped her up, because of his unrestrained lust and perverted actions. As a result, he raped her instead of fortifying her.

Remember the woman in the mirror described at the beginning of this book? She was reaching for her destiny, but ungodly soul ties were pulling her away from it. This is also Tamar's story. As the king's daughter, she had a great future ahead of her and should have been prospering, living, and thriving. But because Amnon had this twisted, perverted thing in his heart that came in through the door of lust, he took hold of his sister, perverted their relationship, formed an ungodly soul tie, and messed her up for the rest of her life! For after Amnon got what he wanted, his innocent little sister became just a woman to him and her life went into a downward tailspin!

The Third Strand of an Ungodly Soul Tie

This leads us to the third strand that makes up an ungodly soul tie: *desolation.* Let's revisit our biblical reference scriptures in II Samuel 13, verses 17 and 20. After Amnon raped Tamar, he called his servants and said, "Put now this [woman] out from me." At this point, Amnon's true colors have been revealed. Verse 20 is the result of his devastating actions: "So Tamar *remained desolate* in her brother Absalom's house." Desolate means to lay waste, to be discarded or empty, barren, and unable to produce. So after Tamar's ordeal with Amnon, she remained tied to the event, leaving her utterly desolate in her other brother Absalom's house.

Interestingly enough, Absalom's name in the Hebrew means "father of peace." But even living in the home of the "father of peace," Tamar still remained barren and unable to produce the rest of her life. She still couldn't move forward into her purpose and destiny, because her ungodly soul tie with Amnon was still pulling her back, controlling her life and tying her down. Tamar was just like our woman in the mirror with the belt around her waist and the strings attached, pulling her back from all God purposed and promised her to be and become.

The Holy Spirit showed me through this study that you and I can be dwelling in the house of the Father of Peace, saved, sanctified, and doing all the right things. We can be in church and have access to the Shekinah glory of God and still be desolate because ungodly soul ties are binding us. Everyone around us can be flourishing and growing in their ministries, prospering in their businesses, living in wonderful health, and awesome relationships, all the while you find yourself in a desolate place all because of an ungodly soul tie. Because of this connection, you feel completely drained, constrained, empty, and barren. Even though God has promised you a wonderful life and destiny, in the midst of all the promises and awesome words of prophecy, you still have barrenness in your soul. Can you say, "Break free to break through?"

"You can't have NOW

until you let go of THEN.

Some NOWs in your life

will definitely be affected

if you don't let go of the

negative THENs

from your past."

-T.L. Campbell

CHAPTER 6

HOW UNGODLY SOUL TIES AFFECT YOUR "NOW"

Let's go back to Tamar. Our scripture reference states Amnon's servants shoved her out of Amnon's chambers and "bolted the door after her." For Amnon the horrible event might have been over, but for Tamar it was a different story. Like Tamar, and if you're anything like me, after the door of the relationship and event you were involved in was "bolted shut," you thought that chapter of your life was closed. You thought you had closed the door to those people who treated you badly and betrayed your trust. You thought you had closed the door to those church people who hurt you and discredited your name. I must tell you, however, that if you are still tied to the relationships or events that formed the ungodly soul ties, knowingly or unknowingly, you will keep being pulled back, keep losing ground, and remain desolate.

If you react negatively in your emotions, or act out in some kind of way that hurts you or those around you every time you think of that person or situation you formed the ungodly soul tie with, that's a good indication you're still attached to him, her, or it. If God sends you a good husband, for example, you can still react to that good man negatively if you had an awful experience with your first husband and you're dragging negative emotions from your first marriage into your second. Or, if God sends you to a new and promising job, you can drive the people in your new office away if the folks at your last job treated you badly and you're transferring the feelings you have toward your former co-workers onto your new co-workers. In either case, the results of your negative reactions are sabotaging relationships and opportunities that are meant to be a blessing to you.

If you're reacting negatively to situations in your life, because you're still bound by an ungodly soul tie, whether it's a past relationship, an event, or a thing, that can affect what God wants to do in your life now! When the Holy Spirit showed me personally how I was responding negatively to life situations because I was connected to ungodly soul ties, He said to me, "Something in your THEN is affecting your NOW." How about you? If you're honest with yourself can you say, "Something in my THEN is affecting my NOW."

The Holy Spirit also said to me, "You can't have NOW until you let go of THEN." Some NOWs in your life will definitely be affected if you don't let go of the negative THENs from your past. Believe it or not, an ungodly soul tie can affect your ability to believe and step out in faith. The Bible teaches, "NOW faith is the substance of things hoped for and the evidence of things not seen."

Your divine inheritance can also be another NOW that's affected by an ungodly soul tie. I John 3:2 says, "NOW are we the sons of God!"

John is not speaking of "sons" from a gender standpoint. Rather, "sons" represent mature believers ready for the Father's inheritance. So if you and I don't sever ungodly soul ties, they can keep us from maturing in God and from experiencing all the Father wants to give us as part of being joint heirs with Christ.

The final NOW that affects you by not letting go of your negative THENs is your destiny. Luke 1:57 says, "NOW Elisabeth's full time came that she should be delivered..." If you are willing to sever your stifling ungodly soul ties, you can freely give birth to the things of God and walk into your destiny. Now let us continue and see what else ungodly soul ties steal from you.

"How many of us have

lost our identities,

because we're still bound

by ungodly soul ties?

Some are still tied to their

ugly divorce, devastating

rape, molestation, and

even racism..."

-T.L. Campbell

CHAPTER 7

WHAT UNGODLY SOUL TIES STEAL FROM YOU

L et's go back to our key scripture passage, II Samuel 13, and look at verses 19 and 20:

19 And Tamar put ashes on her head, and rent her garment of divers colours that [was] on her, and laid her hand on her head, and went on crying.

20 And Absalom her brother said unto her, Hath Amnon thy brother been with thee? but hold now thy peace, my sister:

he [is] thy brother; regard not this thing.
So Tamar remained desolate in her brother
Absalom's house.

Absalom knew immediately that something
devastating had happened to his sister. He
recognized that an ungodly connection had
been made.

Verse 19 says that Tamar rented her coat of
many colours. Rent is a Hebrew word meaning
to tear away, strip off. I believe she did this
because she was tied to the horrible event, not
to mention tied to Amnon by an ungodly soul
tie. Being raped by your brother can't be an easy
thing to shake off and move on from.

Here's the thing about Tamar's robe. The robe
identified who Tamar was in the kingdom, and

she took it off because she felt stripped of who she once was. Many of us have also taken off the glorious robes our Father God gave us because we are still bound by ungodly soul ties. Many have taken off anointings and spiritual mantles, because they're bound to a person, a negative event, an ideology, or a belief system.

Tamar lost her identity. How many of us have lost our identities, because we're still bound by ungodly soul ties? Some are still tied to their ugly divorce, devastating rape, molestation, and even racism. Some are even tied to negative misconceptions that someone else spoke over their life. Are you?

Deep down Tamar lost something priceless. Not only did she lose her sexual purity, because she was a virgin, but she lost something in her spirit that caused her to get out of alignment with God's plan and purpose for her life and seasons of advancement.

I've found in my work as a coach that so many people have lost years or missed seasons, just like Tamar. That's a crucial thing to miss a season. I don't know about you, but I don't want to miss my season(s), especially after I have fasted and prayed, pressed, and interceded for the promises of God to be manifested in my life. But if I'm connected to ungodly soul ties, like Tamar and the woman in the mirror, it's easy to miss seasons if the ungodly soul ties keep pulling me away from what God has prepared for me as He reveals in the mirror of my destiny.

I don't know where you stand with this, but I personally don't want my story to end like Tamar's, -barren ALL the days of my life. I must admit what she went through was very hard. I don't blame her for not initially having the courage to push through her pain. What she went through was terrible, but the truly sad part is that she came back into the house of the "father of peace" and didn't receive the healing, deliverance, and the breakthrough she desperately needed. As a result of the ungodly soul tie, she was unable to tap into and use what was around her so she could get her deliverance. That's why she remained desolate in the house of her brother, Absalom (who happened to be a good, Godly soul tie) for the rest of her life. Can you see how an ungodly soul tie can even affect a good soul tie? Wow!

My friend, do not allow desolation to overtake your life. Ask God, the Father of Peace, to deliver you from all the ungodly soul ties that are sucking the life out of you. When you go to Him and behold His mirror (the Bible and personal words of prophecy), you'll see the wonderful life He has planned for you (read and meditate on Jeremiah 29:11). Don't let fear paralyze you.

Seek help from qualified people around you who can serve as good soul ties in your life and bring you to a place of wholeness and peace. This may mean working with a qualified counselor or therapist for a season. Then once you are brought to that place of healing, work with a certified life coach and move forward in your life. You can do it and it will be worth the time, money, and effort.

Mirror, Mirror on the Wall

A Moment to Reflect

List three things that have been stolen from you as a result of ungodly soul ties.

How can you recover what has been stolen?

"We can't be ignorant of Satan's devices. It's his job to pervert relationships and convert good Godly soul ties into ungodly soul ties in order to misalign you and those you are in relationship with from your God-given purpose and destiny."

-T.L. Campbell

CHAPTER 8

HOW TO IDENTIFY UNGODLY SOUL TIES IN YOUR LIFE

As we move along in our study, I want to encourage you to examine how Tamar's life reflects yours. We can all be affected by the first two strands of an ungodly soul tie, *lust* and *perversion*. We can all have an intense longing to be accepted and loved without being rejected. We can all have an intense longing to walk in power, to be in control, which leads to out-of-balance or perverted relationships.

It's so easy for forbidden lines to be crossed and to form ungodly soul ties with people, even those God sent your way to build you up and fortify you. When some or all the parties involved in the relationship are driven by lust, things can quickly get out of balance and become twisted, and what was meant for good ends up being something harmful or downright evil and toxic. This, my friend, is one of the reasons so many people and relationships are messed up today.

You can form ungodly soul ties with people who were only supposed to be in your life for a season. God will use the relationship as a good soul tie to advance His will and purpose in the lives of you and the other parties involved. When the season for a connection expires according to God's timetable, however, the relationship can unfortunately transform into an ungodly soul tie, because the grace of God for the relationship has lifted. At that point, fleshly lust can slip in and open the door for the relationship to become perverted. Then all the good God desired and purposed to accomplish is diminished, and some or all the parties involved in the relationship are hurtled into despair and left with a bad taste in their mouths. Have you ever experienced that?

I really feel, and know from experience, this is a trick the enemy uses to undermine the purpose of God and the advancement of His will. This is why I so often stress to people not to take the Word of God's admonition as found in I Peter 5:8 (KJV) for granted: "Be sober, be vigilant; because your adversary the devil, as a roaring lion, walketh about, seeking whom he may devour:" Your enemy is seeking ways to impede your growth and progress. He wants to misalign you and throw you off course. He will even pervert a good soul tie if you step out of God's will, timing, and season for the relationship.

One such relationship in my own life that fits this whole "season and timing" issue was a relationship I had with a good friend of mine. She and I had developed a great bond and worked powerfully together as a ministerial tag team. She and I thought we would be God's power team forever! But this wasn't God's ultimate plan. Looking back, I now see we were only brought together for a season as ministerial peers to fortify and build each other up. When this purpose was accomplished in God's timing, we should have separated and moved on to our next phase of development. But we were so driven by our own intense desire (lust) to work together in ministry, we stepped through the door of perversion.

When I say perversion, I must clarify it wasn't anything weird, deviant, and most certainly not of a sexual nature, but things got twisted, because we wanted to do things our way. We misaligned ourselves to God's desire for us in that season by feeding off each other's support instead of depending on God's grace to do His will in ministry. Walking contrary to God's will in the relationship led to it becoming an ungodly soul tie unable to advance the will and purpose of God for each of our lives. This could have left us both at our current levels of development at that time had God not intervened and separated us so we could continue to grow in Him as He purposed for each of us.

This whole perversion thing and the dynamics of it, as it relates to an ungodly soul tie, is worth exploring more deeply. When you allow your soul, (which is your mind, your will, and your emotions) to be connected in a perverted way, whether knowingly or unknowingly, even to things in your past, it can affect your present.

You could be sitting in church worshipping and hearing the Word, then you start to think about somebody you used to be with way back when. Like I mentioned before, it's amazing how something from your THEN can hinder what God wants to give you NOW. You're waiting for your Boaz, but you're still hanging onto Bozo!

This hang-up can be tied to how he used to make you feel and the soulish connection that still ties you to that person. He knew just the right places to touch you physically, emotionally, or both, and that fueled your intense desires. This lust then opened the door to perversion, especially if the soulish connection led to bodies connecting in a sexual relationship outside the honorable boundary of marriage. Unless the ungodly soul tie is broken, you can easily be pulled and drawn away from the direction God is calling you. Can you say, "break free to break through?"

Back to II Samuel 13:11: "…he took hold of her, and said unto her, Come lie with me, my sister." In Hebrew, "Come lie with me" means to be intimately connected. I don't know if this includes you, but many people have connected intimately with things, people, and ideals that cause them to give birth to things in their lives God never intended. When you're intimate with a person, a seed is planted. If you and the seed stay connected long enough, it begins to grow. So we're talking about breaking free so we can break through. In life, you and I have to cut loose from all the things we're connected to that pull us away from God, and enter into greater intimacy with the Father. He knows what's best, and I am determined to follow Him. How about you?

I can't stress enough how anything that's leading you astray from the will and purpose of God can very well be the result of an ungodly soul tie, especially if all the telltale signs of lust and perversion are present. If you feel you're being manipulated in any way, then you need to check the connection. In most cases the root of an ungodly soul tie is control, and Satan will use the control to take advantage of the people involved in almost any type of relationship. Satan especially likes to use the relationships closest to you.

If, for example, you're an adult and your mother or father is still telling you what to do and pushing negative buttons in your life, that relationship can easily become twisted. Once it becomes twisted, a relationship like this, which is meant to be a good soul tie, can easily convert to an ungodly soul tie if things aren't put in proper perspective. If God is telling you to go one way, and your mother or father is telling you to go the other, the relationship may become perverted and out of order. God is supposed to be your head, not your momma or your daddy. I'm not talking about not seeking wise counsel, but about not allowing others to control you and your life.

This scenario can be flipped to where the child is the one manipulating the parent. In any case, we can't be ignorant of Satan's devices. It's his job to pervert relationships and convert good Godly soul ties into ungodly soul ties in order to misalign you and those you are in relationship with from your God-given purpose and destiny.

I'm finding even relationships between spiritual parents and spiritual sons and daughters in a church or ministry setting can get out of balance when any one of the parties lusts for control. Like I mentioned before, once someone opens the door of perversion and the relationship gets twisted, the relationship transforms into an ungodly soul tie. As a result, some or all the parties involved leave the relationship desolate, barren, and non-productive. Do you see what I'm saying?

Even a toxic, controlling church or religious system can lead to the formation of ungodly soul ties, especially if the institution's traditions and ideologies are perverted and hold their parishioners captive. When that happens, the parishioners are often left spiritually, emotionally, and physically constrained, drained, desolate, and barren. Come on say it with me, "break free to break through."

"For years I couldn't understand why I was stuck in a holding pattern of non-productivity. Just like the woman in the mirror, I couldn't understand what caused me to be pulled away from my God-given purpose and destiny..."

-T.L. Campbell

CHAPTER 9

MY STORY:
A STARTLING REVELATION

I can speak so freely and insightfully about ungodly soul ties because I had some myself. About twelve years ago, I started asking God why I wasn't growing in certain areas of my life. When the answer came to me, I was a bit surprised. The Holy Spirit told me I was experiencing barrenness as a result of an ungodly soul tie with someone from my past. Even more surprising, it was an ungodly soul tie with a spiritual leader who I once had great respect for and considered a father figure in my life.

I will spare you all the ugly details, but the relationship ended when the spiritual leader crossed the boundary of our father and daughter relationship and approached me inappropriately. He not only betrayed my trust with his inappropriate actions, but he also betrayed the trust of my husband, who also considered him a father figure. All I could say then was, "Wow! I didn't see that coming." My husband and I were left totally devastated. Needless to say, the relationship with the leader ended after this unfortunate event.

I can't begin to tell you how this event negatively affected not only my life, but the life of my immediate family who trusted the leader too. For years I was bitter and angry, because when I took the proper steps according to biblical protocol to bring this leader's actions to church leadership, nothing was done. Without proper recourse for this leader, over the years he continued to approach other women in the ministry inappropriately, and left many families devastated.

After this heartbreaking event, I spent several years desolate emotionally and spiritually. I still wanted a relationship with God, but I kicked the church and my call to ministry to the curb and went into five years of isolation. This was a big no-no and a trick of the enemy, because in order for us as believers to grow properly and flourish, we not only need God, but we also need the Body of Christ. Ephesians 4:16 (NLT) says, "He makes the whole body fit together perfectly. As each part does its own special work, it helps the other parts grow, so that the whole body is healthy and growing and full of love."

While being connected to the Body of Christ is crucial and essential, I chose to isolate myself, because I was hurt deeply. I will share more about the subject of disconnecting from those God joined me to in another volume of the *Woman in the Mirror Empowerment Series*™, titled *Woman in the Mirror: The Walls Must Fall*, but let me bring this point to mind. Just like Tamar, my unfortunate event left me desolate and barren. I lost so much ground over the years, because I let what happened to my husband and me dominate me. I can't begin to tell you how many God-appointed opportunities I missed, because I chose to remain connected to the devastating event brought on by an ungodly soul tie.

Like Tamar, I too, stripped off my royal spiritual garments, mantles of power, and authority given to me by Father God. I was the woman in the mirror with the belt tied around her waist and the ropes pulling her out of the presence, will, and purpose of God. Like I said before, I was doing all the right things: reading my Bible, paying my tithes, and giving my offerings, but I was going nowhere fast, because the ungodly soul ties in my life kept pulling me back! Can you say with me, "Break free to break through"?

The Holy Spirit revealed to me, however, that in my situation, the lust component that formed the ungodly soul tie was a two-way street. This revelation blew my socks off! To begin with, the leader still had unresolved issues with sexual lust, and even though the Holy Spirit revealed to me that I didn't have a problem in any way with sexual lust, I did have an intense desire for a father and to be accepted by him.

Growing up without a strong father figure left me with a father deficit, father wounds, and father hunger (more about that later in another volume in the series). As a result, I had a void in my life that I wanted to fill so badly that I was blinded to what was headed my way and let my spiritual guard down. I was totally blindsided by this. If I had seen it coming, I would have avoided it like the plague!

The Holy Spirit showed me that because the leader had a serious hidden problem with sexual lust, he preyed on my neediness and opened the door to pervert our once-wholesome spiritual father-daughter relationship. Once the door of perversion was opened, of course the relationship between the leader, my husband, and myself was never the same. The once-good soul tie quickly converted to an ungodly soul tie, which left my husband and me (and many others whose trust was crushed) completely desolated.

It took some time to heal and forgive, which by the grace of God I was able to do eventually, but the leader who betrayed my husband and me kept showing up in my dreams while I slept, even though consciously I wasn't thinking about him at all. From time to time I would even feel the leader's presence in the room with me, which was so bizarre!

As I sought God about these strange occurrences, the Holy Spirit showed me that because I had not severed the ungodly soul tie with the leader, there was still a level of turbulence in my soul, and this disturbance was being played out in my dreams. I also felt the Holy Spirit revealed to me how the leader was crossing the line spiritually and using the intact soul tie as a connection to astral project his spirit and gain access into my presence, unbeknownst to me (or so he thought, but the Holy Spirit had given me the heads up). I know this may sound strange to some, but evil spiritual activity like this goes on all the time. This is why you and I can't be ignorant of Satan's devices and those who work in conjunction with his plan to sabotage the destinies of others. (II Corinthians 2:11).

For years I couldn't understand why I was stuck in a holding pattern of non-productivity. Just like the woman in the mirror, I couldn't understand what caused me to be pulled away from my God-given purpose and destiny. I couldn't understand why the leader kept showing up in my dreams since I had sought

God to forgive the leader for what he had done, and I had consciously moved on. Even stranger than that, I couldn't understand why I was sensing his presence in the room with me from time to time. Well, I got my answer!

Once what was happening in the spirit was revealed, and the Holy Spirit instructed me how to sever the ungodly soul tie, and the dreams and weird occurrences stopped completely. Thank God for that! I was so grateful the Holy Spirit, with such precision, revealed the "real deal" and set me on a path to healing and freedom. God wanted His best for me, and when I asked for help He gave me divine insight. My time to "break free to break through" had arrived!

At this point you may be thinking about the different relationships or occurrences in your life that have the telltale signs of being an ungodly soul tie. You may feel like I did: *I'm that woman in the mirror, who is being pulled back each time she tries to get closer to God or advance in life.* Your day of liberation has arrived, too. It's God's will that you be set free so you can be all He desires for you to be. God did it for me and He can do it for you, too. In the next chapter, I will share the necessary steps you can take to break free to break through. Once you take these steps, you will open the door to the endless possibilities the Father has set before you to have a prosperous and fulfilled life.

Sometimes It's Not Your Fault

Not all ungodly soul ties formed in our lives are our fault. Sometimes we get caught up in other people's madness, just like Tamar got caught up in Amnon's madness and ended up a casualty because of his twisted desires and actions.

Multitudes of people are entangled by ungodly soul ties because of other people's lust and perversion. Sometimes an ungodly soul tie can be formed as a result of a rape, an abortion, or some type of abuse. Being tied to any of these traumatic events can leave you desolate, especially if guilt and shame are part of the equation. Then, just like the woman in the mirror, every time you try to draw close to God and embrace your purpose and destiny in Him, the tragic event keeps pulling you away. I want to declare to you, "It's time to break free!" You owe it to yourself. You can do it just like I did.

"*The ungodly soul tie must be revealed. The lights have to come on. You have to wake from your sleep, your slumber; realize the position you're in; and acknowledge the ungodly soul ties in your life.*"

-T.L. Campbell

CHAPTER 10

HOW TO SEVER
UNGODLY SOUL TIES

When the Holy Spirit begins revealing the ungodly soul ties in your life, you may ask yourself, "How do I sever them?" The Holy Spirit answered this question when He led me to a study in Isaiah 52:1-2 (KJV) and said to me, "There are three cuts or steps that you have to make to sever the ties that bind." Let's look at that passage of scripture:

1 Awake, awake; put on thy strength, O Zion; put on thy beautiful garments, O

Jerusalem, the holy city: for henceforth there shall no more come into thee the uncircumcised and the unclean.

2 Shake thyself from the dust; arise, [and] sit down, O Jerusalem: loose thyself from the bands of thy neck, O captive daughter of Zion.

Now I want to share the same scripture passage with a spiritual amplification from the Holy Spirit as it relates to our subject. The amplification can be seen in the brackets.

Verse 1: Awake, awake; put on thy strength, O Zion; [it's talking to the church or you personally, the woman who is standing in front of the mirror] put on thy beautiful garments [the wonderful kingdom garments Father God initially clothed you with, but you took them off as a result of the ungodly soul ties] O Jerusalem, the holy city: for henceforth there shall no more come into thee the uncircumcised and the unclean [the perverted and twisted].

Verse 2: Shake thyself from the dust; [from people or things that serve as ungodly soul ties in your life] arise, [and] sit down, O Jerusalem: loose thyself from the bands of thy neck, [free yourself from the ungodly soul ties of your mind, your will, your emotions, etc.] O captive daughter of Zion.

With this amplification of the two verses, the scripture passage comes alive and hits home! At least it did for me.

Now let's look at what you have to do to sever these ungodly soul ties. The first thing you need to do is found in verse 1: "Awake, awake."

Cut # 1

"Awake, awake." The first cut to sever the ungodly soul tie involves revelation.

The ungodly soul tie must be revealed. The lights have to come on. You have to wake from your sleep, your slumber; realize the position you're in; and acknowledge the ungodly soul ties in your life. This is a crucial key to your breakthrough. You have to take an inventory of your relationships, connections, and associations, and evaluate them. In doing so, ask yourself these questions:

1. Is this relationship, connection, or association a Godly soul tie or an ungodly soul tie?

2. Is this relationship, connection, or association mutually beneficial for all parties involved?

3. Is this relationship, connection, or association advancing the will and purpose of God in my life or the other person's life?

4. Am I still tied to a past event that's holding me back?

5. Am I tied to a constraining institution or belief system that's holding me back?

The second thing you need to do to sever ungodly soul ties is found in verse 2: "Shake thyself from the dust; arise."

Cut #2

"Shake thyself from the dust; arise." The second cut to sever ungodly soul ties involves spiritual warfare.

With this cut, you have to roll up your sleeves and prepare to fight! I don't mean fighting in the natural with slaps and punches, for Ephesians 6:12 (NLT) says: "For we are not fighting against flesh-and-blood enemies, but against evil rulers and authorities of the unseen world, against mighty powers in this dark world, and against evil spirits in the heavenly places."

Rather, Isaiah 52:2 tells us to "shake thyself from the dust; arise." That particular word *shake* in the Hebrew language means "to overthrow," "to toss off," or "to throw down." Basically you've got to "throw down in the spirit" to sever ungodly soul ties, because they are rooted in the spiritual realm. You can't fight with your natural hands and war in the natural, although in some cases you may have to physically remove yourself from the connection.

Be aware that some ungodly soul ties are strongly rooted ties that are governed by manipulating evil master spirits. So to sever such ties, you have to "arise," or ascend in the spirit and do spiritual warfare! Engage on a spiritual level by using the spiritual weapons of prayer, intercession, and fasting.

When you pray, you are communicating with God and seeking His help and power to sever the ungodly soul ties. The next weapon in your arsenal is intercession. Intercession takes you deeper in your efforts to sever deeply rooted soul ties. Intercession involves praying in the spirit using your prayer language, or as some call it, "praying in tongues."

When you pray in tongues, you are allowing the Holy Spirit to pray through you. That's what makes praying in tongues so powerful and effective. The Holy Spirit knows exactly what to pray regarding the ungodly soul tie. With absolute precision, He zeros in on the ties that bind and intercedes on your behalf. To back up what I'm saying, let's read Romans 8:26-27 (NLT):

26 And the Holy Spirit helps us in our weakness. For example, we don't know what God wants us to pray for. But the Holy Spirit prays for us with groanings that cannot be expressed in words.

27 And the Father who knows all hearts knows what the Spirit is saying, for the Spirit pleads for us believers in harmony with God's own will.

You can't lose if you allow the Holy Spirit to wage war against the evil forces behind the ungodly soul ties in your life. This is why it's so important to seek God for the precious and powerful indwelling gift of the Holy Spirit, with evidence of speaking in tongues. The Holy Spirit living within you wants to come alongside you and assist in the fight. He is a bona fide spiritual ally, through whom you can activate strategic spiritual weapons that will get the job done!

Another strategic spiritual weapon that will assist you in severing ungodly soul ties is fasting. Fasting commonly involves abstaining from food for a set period of time and is an effective tool to dismantle the works of darkness and sever the ties that bind, especially when you couple it with prayer and intercession.

Jesus spoke of the effectiveness of fasting and prayer in Matthew 17:14-21 when He responded to a father's desperate plea for his demon-bound son, who was constantly being controlled by an evil spirit who "took hold of him," caused him to have uncontrollable epileptic fits, and cast him into the fire and water. The father asked

Jesus' disciples to help his son, but they couldn't. After Jesus delivered the boy from the controlling spirit, He told the disciples in Matthew 17:21(NKJV), "However, this kind does not go out except by prayer and fasting."

Just like the man's son in Matthew 17, you as a child of God can be bound by ungodly soul ties that control your life. Just like the boy, through the power of ungodly control, manipulation, and perverted motives, you, too, can constantly find yourself in peril as you are cast into the harmful fires and waters of life because of ungodly soul ties.

It's going to take fasting to break the ungodly soul tie with that man or woman you slept with. It's going to take some fasting and prayer to get those people out of your system who hurt you badly and did you wrong in your family, on your job, or even in your church. I know you thought you were over that person(s) and the whole life-shattering incident, but if seeing him, her, or them still bothers you, it's a good indication there is still an ungodly soul tie intact. You will know you're free when you no longer react when you see that person, when you feel a freedom from the pull of the ungodly soul tie and its control, and when you no longer feel you and your emotions being pulled in the wrong direction, like the woman in the mirror.

Now on to the third and final cut to sever the ungodly soul tie, which is found in verse 2: "sit down."

Cut#3

"Sit down." The third cut to sever an ungodly soul tie involves learning to rest in God and the finished work of Christ. That is the key to maintaining your freedom.

The Holy Spirit shared with me that completely breaking free from an ungodly soul tie requires that you and I cease from our labors, from our need to be validated, and from our need to have others' approval, and just rest in the I AM (who is God). We must seek to become one with the I AM. In the I AM we can truly come to know who we are and do what the Father created us to do for His purpose. No longer will we have to live a life of desolation and despair, like Tamar.

Isaiah 51:3 says, "For the LORD shall comfort Zion: he will comfort all her waste places; and he will make her wilderness like Eden, and her desert like the garden of the LORD; joy and gladness shall be found therein, thanksgiving, and the voice of melody."

This scripture indicates it's God's desire for you to live in peace. He also wants to transform all the desolate places of your life into fruitful gardens of joy and gladness. From the sound of this scripture, the Father wants you to break free from the ties that bind and release a glorious song in your heart. This is God's highest will and purpose for your life. He doesn't want you dwelling in the wasteland and remaining desolate in the Father's house. He already made provision for your deliverance; for in that verse

He said, "For the Lord shall comfort Zion: he will comfort all her waste places;" (meaning all the places in your life that are desolate because of ungodly soul ties. He will bring you rest).

He goes onto say, "...he will make her wilderness like Eden." This sounds like a turnaround to me! Things in your life will become fruitful – no longer will you be barren. No longer will you be tossed to and fro like the woman in the mirror, pulled in every direction. When the Lord is finished delivering you, you will have clear focus and clear direction because you will be able to behold in the mirror the image of the Lord in true intimacy, and you will be changed from glory, to glory, to glory. In-to-me-you-see – the more you see, the more you can become and obtain.

The scripture also says the dry places of your life will be like "the garden of the Lord." When you sever your ungodly soul ties, God is going to come and pick fruit from your tree. I even believe according to Isaiah 61:3-4 that God is going to dramatically transform your desolate places so you will, in turn, give fruits of righteousness to those around you and repair the damage of generations before you:

> 3 To appoint unto them that mourn in Zion, to give unto them beauty for ashes, the oil of joy for mourning, the garment of praise for the spirit of heaviness; that they might be called trees of righteousness, the planting of the LORD, that he might be glorified.

> 4 And they shall build the old wastes, they shall raise up the former desolations, and

they shall repair the waste cities, the desolations of many generations.

I'm talking about breaking free to break through! Your breaking free is not only about you; it's about the purpose and the plan of God within you that will affect other people, too. God is going to make you His garden and use you as a good soul tie to others. Glory to God – hallelujah!

Our key scripture for Cut #3 (Isaiah 51:3) concludes by saying the Lord is going to give you joy and gladness, and thanksgiving will be found therein. When you sever the ungodly soul ties in your life, God will put a melody in your heart so your life will become a melody unto Him. It's your time to "break free to break through!"

"When you sever the ungodly soul ties in your life, it's going to be critical that you stay vigilant throughout your life. Watch your connections..."

-T.L. Campbell

CHAPTER 11

A FINAL WORD AND PRAYER

So now you know what you have to do to sever ungodly soul ties. In conclusion, I want to come into agreement with you and decree and declare that every ungodly soul tie in your life be broken. But before we pray I want to encourage you to remain watchful. Even after you experience the breaking of an ungodly soul tie, you have to maintain your freedom. Galatians 5:1 says, "Stand fast therefore in the liberty wherewith Christ hath made us free, and be not entangled again with the yoke of bondage."

When you sever the ungodly soul ties in your life, it's going to be critical that you stay vigilant throughout your life. Watch your connections; watch who and what you connect with and who and what connects with you. Be determined in your mind that you're not going to let anyone or anything keep you from true intimacy with God, your true identity in Him, and from your God-given purpose and destiny.

Let's pray:

Lord, we thank you today for my friend and the wonderful plan you have for them. Lord God, we thank you for this word and pray that its liberating power causes them to break free. Father, we thank you for the breakthrough, because we want to be in the position where we can be used for your glory.

Lord, I pray right now that you would bless my sisters and brothers. Father, they have heard the word, and I pray right now that You allow it to take root, even in the hidden parts and secret crevices of their minds, O God.

Lord, I pray right now that you would cause your power and your anointing to sever every ungodly soul tie that's connected to them today. Father, I ask you to sever every ungodly soul tie, past and present, that's keeping them from being the mighty vessel of honor you've called them to be. Lord, I pray right now that you release an anointing in their lives that will sever the ties that bind. Lord God, send your breakthrough anointing into their lives, destroying every yoke of darkness. Sever every yoke of the enemy that seeks to enslave and imprison your child. I declare and decree every incapacitating tie is broken in the name of Jesus.

Father, based on the power you vested in me, I now release Godly soul ties into their lives. Let them connect with people, groups, ideals, and belief systems that will advance your will and your purpose in their lives today. In the name of Jesus, I declare and decree this word and prayer will take root, grow, and bring forth much fruit in their lives. May they become a Garden of Eden and serve as good soul ties to those around them in the name of Jesus, Amen.

Tarsha L. Campbell is a dynamic, God-appointed Woman of Destiny! God has called Tarsha to teach His people who He is and their true identity in Him. With this mandate, she humbly serves as a powerful bible teacher, inspirational speaker, certified empowerment and destiny coach, entrepreneur, and business and ministry consultant.

Since childhood, Tarsha has possessed a love for the truth and the meat of God's Word. It is through this love that God has birthed life-altering prophetic teachings that are reaching people from all walks of life around the world. Tarsha is most known for the powerful teaching series, *The Woman in the Mirror*, which has imparted life to those who desire to walk in their true identity in Christ. Her unique, illustrated teaching style has allowed many to see and understand what the Father is saying with complete clarity, practical application, and unprecedented spiritual breakthrough!

Tarsha is a published author. Her book titles include: *Called and Chosen: A Study Guide to Ministry, Help! I've Been Called By God: Easy Steps to Preparing and Delivering a Message, 5 Qualities of a Woman of Destiny,*

Woman in the Mirror: A Case of Mistaken Identity and *Woman in the Mirror: Ungodly Soul Ties - Break Free to Break Through.*

God's vision for Tarsha's life also includes helping other ministers and authors publish their writings, so she has launched Dominionhouse Publishing & Design, a publishing and graphic design firm dedicated to publishing *The Good News* with divine ingenuity and creative excellence. Tarsha is also the Executive Director of Revealed International Women's Empowerment Network, Inc., an organization dedicated to helping women unveil their God-given identity, potential, purpose, & destiny. The organization's lifetime mission is to help 100,000 women find their life purpose.

Tarsha believes there is nothing we can't do if we learn to tap into the divine mind of God and walk in who we really are in Him. She resides in the Central Florida area with her husband of 27 years and their two children.

Connect with her on:
www.facebook.com/tarsha.campbell
www.twitter.com/CoachTarsha
www.instagram.com/TarshaCampbell
www.TarshaCampbellEmpowers.com
www.connecttoempower.com

CONTACT THE AUTHOR

Please email or write the author with any comments you may have. You are also welcome to contact her for bookings. As the Holy Spirit leads, Tarsha is available for book club presentations, book signings, or speaking engagements for your church or organization (women's ministries, women's clubs, conferences, workshops, retreats, and seminars). She is available for ministerial and business presentations, each developed specifically for your group or event.

Contact her at:
tarsha@TarshaCampbellEmpowers.com

For bookings visit:
www.TarshaCampbellEmpowers.com
or www.UngodlySoulTies.com

P.O. Box 681938
Orlando, Florida 32868
407.703.4800

I love Coaching! My life has been radically transformed as a result of it and now as a Certified Life and Empowerment Coach I want to help you!
—Tarsha L. Campbell

Do the following describe you?

- Lack of vision
- Desire motivation
- Unable to focus on goals
- Living life without passion
- Overwhelmed by everyday life
- Seeking fulfillment and purpose
- Feeling out of touch or out of sync
- Experiencing spiritual death cycles
- Having trouble embracing change
- Stuck in an unproductive rut/going in circles

If any of these things describe you, coaching can benefit you. Get in sync with God's will for your life. Coaching can help you reclaim balance, control, motivation, purpose, vision, and ultimately destiny fulfillment! Help is just a click away at:

www.revealedinternational.com
For more information email:
info@revealedinternational.com

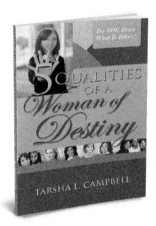

Have You Been Called?

Do You Know Who You Are?

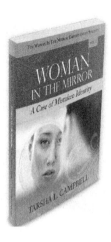

Now available from DOMINIONHOUSE
Great for individual or group study

Get ready to embark upon a journey of extreme liberation and extraordinary healing! This book is designed to help you identify and demolish misconceptions and strongholds that distort your true identity in Christ. Get ready to find the real you and be placed on a path to divine fulfillment. Get ready to be set free!

Order your copy today! Available at:

www.TarshaCampbellEmpowers.com
amazon.com, barnesandnoble.com
and other fine book retailers
Just ask for the book.

The Mission of
DOMINIONHOUSE
Publishing & Design, LLC

The Lord gave the word: great was
the company of those that published it.
(Psalms 68:11)

****

DOMINIONHOUSE Publishing & Design offers quality, custom publishing products and design services catered exclusively to your needs at affordable prices. From concept to fulfillment, it is our commitment to work cooperatively with entrepreneurs, corporations, organizations, ministries, and authors, to creatively bring your vision to life with excellence!

At DOMINIONHOUSE, we're passionate about making you look good, and helping you leave your mark in the marketplace and beyond.

For more information about book publishing and our graphic design services, visit:
www.mydominionhouse.com

My Personal Reflections

_____

_____

_____

_____

_____

_____

_____

_____

_____

_____

_____

How precious are your thoughts about
me, O God. They cannot be numbered.

Psalms 139:17 (NIV)

CPSIA information can be obtained at www.ICGtesting.com
Printed in the USA
BVOW11s0338030316

438764BV00008B/80/P